Donkey Press
P.O. Box 20583
New York, N.Y. 10021-0071

Printed in the United States of America
ISBN 0-9650535-0-4

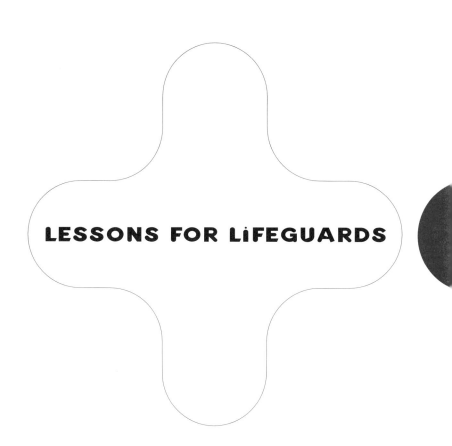

LESSONS FOR LiFEGUARDS

DEDICATION

This book is dedicated to my family:

*my wife June whose love, grace, and nurturing
make life easy;*

*my son Chris whose encouragement propels me
(Donkey Press was his idea);*

*my daughter Courtney and son-in-law Ilario whose belief
in my life's work sustains me;*

*my parents Grace and Jim Carrera who continue to teach
me important lessons about family;*

*my brothers Sal and Jim and their families; and all the
Flexners who
cheer me on in every venture.*

ACKNOWLEDGMENTS

Mary Beth Caschetta, the book's editor, is a gifted and creative writer; her candor, insights, and encouragement kept me on track and helped make the original idea a reality. Abby Jochnowitz and Victor Hunt are the remarkable creative team who designed the book, and Deborah K. Miller Forest worked diligently to find the right printer and facilitate production. Lauren Halye patiently transcribed and typed the original manuscript.

Many thanks to Tom for generosity and support. I am also deeply appreciative of Pat, Iris, Lorna, Katherine, Shavon, Kathy G., Sal, Felipe, and Zranwea – faithful friends and effective co-workers.

Thanks to The Children's Aid Society for providing me with the opportunity to work with the young people and families they serve.

In the summer of 1977, I was fortunate enough to attend "Meditations on Caring" a speech given by Henri J.M. Nouwen at St. Jeromes College in Ontario. My notes on Father Nouwen's presentation remain useful and inspiring. Additionally, *The Spiritual Life of Children* by Robert Coles (Houghton Mifflin, 1990) informed some of my early views.

Finally and always, sincere gratitude to all the teens with whom I have worked over the years; their problems, defeats, aspirations and triumphs are alive in these pages. My invaluable experience with young people helped form my view on what teens need from us, ultimately leading me to write *Lessons for Lifeguards*.

CONTENTS

PREFACE

This book centers on the belief that those of us entrusted with the privilege of access to vulnerable young people must provide for their care and guidance with renewed vigor and determination. Much of what is offered in the following essays, reflections, and "urgings" are unorthodox and risky. You will find no science here; science is difficult to apply to teens who display both an admirable capacity for reason and a frightening inclination toward irrationality as they head toward personality integration, a process that is dizzying for even the most experienced worker. I know because I have stood in your shoes. I, like so many of you, have experienced joy and fulfillment one day, and then, for weeks, felt so much profound despair and defeat that it was almost impossible to get up and go to work.

What you will find in these pages is experienced, practical advice offered within a context of genuine care for teens.

It is my belief that unorthodox and daring pre-vention interventions are essential because orthodox approaches have clearly failed; our best thinking and our best efforts have got us where we are today. In that light, we can be sure that without changing, no change will occur.

We have experienced our own teenage years, and some of us have vicariously experienced the teenage years of our own children; yet, few profession-als truly remember what it was like to be a teen; few can precisely recall the rapid mood swings, the valleys and peaks. When I look at teens, and when I work with them, I see that through their behavior and struggles they are trying to tell us what is happening in society today. It is our privilege – no, our calling – to listen to what they are saying.

Remember this: our best thinking and our best efforts

got us to where we are today.

———

After all is said and done, much is said

and little is done.

WHERE WE ARE TODAY

THE NATIONAL DEBT AND OTHER TRAGEDIES ABOUT TEENS

This is a commentary about our national debt – not the ever-increasing deficit over which the politicians fret, not the rolling numbers on the huge, lighted billboard in New York City which move so quickly even the quickest eyes cannot follow. No, I am referring to a different national debt, one of staggering personal importance. The national debt I speak about is the 1,300 teens who give birth every day in America, the 1,100 teens who have a pregnancy termination every day in America, the 600 teens who are infected with syphilis and gonorrhea every day in America, and the 3 million teens who contract a sexually transmitted infection each year in America. The national debt I want you to think about is the 2,200 teens who drop out of school every day in America, the 5,000 teens who are assaulted every day in America. The fifteen young people who die every day due to firearms. Every day in America, HIV infection occurs in adolescents in growing numbers; so does suicide, substance abuse and alcoholism, and random senseless violence of all kinds.

The difference between this national debt and our fiscal national debt is that this one has faces; it has feelings; it has a family, a future. This national debt has a human toll. This debt is a national tragedy, costing the country hope and lives that are incalculable. The senseless, tragic loss of young people is our true national debt, and the numbers are mounting.

A tally of this loss cannot be lit on a city billboard for everyone to see; instead, it is reflected in the eyes of our sons and daughters, our grand-children. The many, many young people who comprise such a haunting, human debt may never have an opportunity to realize their gifts and talents; for many, their own unique qualities will never have the chance to bloom. They may never know what it is like to use such treasures to benefit themselves, their families, their communities, and their country.

The forces facing young people, stacking the odds against them, are the same forces that spur the splintering of the American family, and lead to a *cul-de-sac* of desperation, fatalism, and despair. Young people are aware of the result: pain and struggle. The specter of hopelessness in them is daunting; it looms large, surrounding them, limiting their aspirations, their possibilities for success. I have heard the haunting voices of countless young people say, "There is no hope. There is no one who values me. There is no one who cares." Is it any wonder that some adolescents, instead of becoming industrious, responsible, and hopeful, seek short-term impulsive fulfillment, use intercourse as a coping mechanism, use substances to anesthetize their feelings and show little value for themselves or for others? These dangerous behaviors employed by many young people today are simply the natural outcome of a deep emptiness experienced every day in America.

The numbers we can rattle off concerning the problems of young people in our communities and throughout our country are indeed staggering, but they do not reflect the core ills we face when working with teens. They are merely the symptoms of something deeper and more complex, the yield of grave forces and factors which have fueled the problems of youth for centuries, generations, decades, and years. I am speaking about such deep-rooted evils as hatred, prejudice, and racism. When a teen we work with is treated differently, is offered fewer opportunities, is approached pessimistically, or is handled with lower expectations due to the color of his or her skin, we are contributing to the national debt and to the core problems which plague this nation. Such an approach on our part is deeply felt by teens, and these wounds affect every aspect of their development, producing feelings of fatalism, creating beliefs like, "I'm going nowhere," and "No one really cares." These feelings and beliefs formed by insidious racism reinforce behaviors that range from apathy to irresponsibility. We must not expect less of any adolescent; we must never treat teens as if they have no or little potential.

Institutional racism constitutes the central moral agony of our times. For decades now, politicians and social policy experts have been mistaken: racism not drugs is our greatest addiction. As a nation, we are at once racially obsessed and fatigued, a problem which will sink us as a culture if it is allowed to continue unchallenged.

The other core forces underwriting our tragic, human national debt include societal antipathy and hatred according to gender, class, and sexual orientation; the fragmentation of the family; and an absence of genuine caring. Together with substandard housing, unequal educational opportunities, and inadequate health care, these deep societal ills will cause us to lose many, many more of our nation's children.

When faced with a young person who seems not to care, who is hostile or antagonistic, it is crucial to remember the long-standing forces which have created the context, which have encouraged these negative, frustrating attitudes. Too many young people are born, nurtured, and raised in unhealthy soil, offering them few nutrients; then, once grown, the adolescents are left to overcome the problems these factors produced at the very same time that they are blamed for them. The difficulties we face in our work with teens are the products of environmental vectors, which have greatly damaged and affected their "developmental soil." It is not the gene-pool or the color of skin of young people that makes our work in helping them so difficult. It is not that they choose apathy, self-depreciation, and hostility. No, these are merely an outgrowth of teens' concrete life experience in the soil where they grow. These are the outcomes of our national debt.

Other Teen Tragedies

We have nothing to be proud of concerning the circumstances of teens in America and nothing much to pass on to the next generation. It is often difficult to think about what the 21st Century will be like for young people. Unless we address the core problems constituting this deep spiritual illness and unless we resolve to challenge and change, then the situation for young people today in America will remain grim.

Our response to the grave situation facing teens, this national debt, has taken the stairs, while the problems of teens are taking the elevator. I can tell you this much: it is our best thinking and our best efforts which have gotten us where we are today. As practitioners, policy-makers, and concerned citizens, we must face facts: our best programs have not reduced this human debt. In fact, every traditional approach we have used to quell the rising tide of tragedies affecting teens has failed miserably. Orthodoxy has failed. Continuing to enshrine traditional ways of working with young people, traditional ways of providing services to adolescents, and traditional ways of educating them is blind and irresponsible. We cannot continue to do things the way they have always been done: it is clear that if we do what we always do, we will get what we have always gotten – poor results.

And yet, for some reason that I cannot understand, people who work with teens seem to refuse to surrender their long-held traditional views and approaches, even though these orthodox methods – perhaps effective once – have failed us in our work today. They have not significantly provided the kind of direction and hope which young people today need so desperately. For instance, can we truly take seriously a proposal for midnight basketball? Can we truly believe that this approach will act as a vaccine for poor teen males? We would be so much further ahead, if we changed our thinking and understood that low-income young men can do more than just play ball. It is time to abandon the idea that a basketball, or any other quick fix, will positively influence life behaviors. If we truly want to help young people, we can do so during the work day, at our employment centers, our career or vocational clinics, our offices or at their schools and community centers. We can help by being present, stable, generous, and caring, not by encouraging basketball, or any other game, at midnight.

Is it any wonder that the doorway we must

pass through in order to reach young people is so narrow? Frequently, the door, which is open just a crack – enough for us to see inside – is slammed shut as we make our approach and intend to step through to deliver our help. Sometimes, the door is slammed because whoever was there before us walked through with promises, but no real change. This is often historically the case. You know the scenario: groups of young people and families with education, housing, health-care, and employment problems are asked to participate in programs that offer nothing about how to prepare themselves to meet these challenges and change their lives. Instead, such groups in need are given information about the newest technology for family planning. Imagine what that must feel like. To have all those needs, to be desperate for help, for food, for shelter, for work, for money, and to be told instead about Norplant and Depo. And then we walk away and wonder what went wrong, or feel confirmed that the audience was already hostile before we ever got there, or we feel insulted when an accusation of genocide emerges.

In the mean time, educators are producing yet more videos, and policy-makers continue to argue for punishment, threats, and sanctions for those young people who do not comply. Government officials and parents clamor for answers and resolution. Their anxiety and pressure are directed at us, and we try to respond by implementing more educational interventions and curricula. But that same stale thinking and rhetoric got us to where we are today. The same unproductive air of blaming teens for their problems surrounds us.

Incantations abound: "If only they knew the facts," or "Teach 'em what they need to know." We have tried desperately to teach our way out of our problems, only to find that, this time, at this moment in history, we cannot teach our way out of this morass. We cannot merely provide information through a hastily developed curriculum targeting vulnerable ages or stages in adolescence. We cannot simply hire some semi-trained specialist to come into our schools or neighborhoods to do away with the offending symptom. But again and again, this is what educators and policy makers do. There are curricula from alcohol abuse to HIV infection to pregnancy prevention and violence intervention – none can singly stem the tide of the tragedies facing youth.

No, this lack of innovation in our work will

not help solve our problems, will not heal wounds, or dry tears, or provide a future, or guarantee a job or college admission. This traditional thinking will not lessen the numbers of lives we are failing to save. *Status quo*, no change, equilibrium are hurting the neediest. No slick educational intervention, no video, no role-play is sufficient alone.

It is time to forget about tinkering or tuning up old programs; a complete overhaul is required in the form of a top-to-bottom radical change in philosophy, expectations, attitudes and practices. It is time for each worker to reject convention and seek out young people, time to do anything and everything to save a teen's life, just as a parent would be singular in his or her devotion to save a child. It is time to put aside the talking, and meeting, and planning, and arguing – all tantamount to trying to jump start the old engine. We need a new engine, for our old ones have failed us, and the rescue operation has been stalled. In the meantime, the maelstrom continues swirling, lifting up teens with its speed and power damaging and destroying their lives.

It may even be time to abandon our newest program, freshly printed brochure, latest slick curriculum, since many of these simply extend our old ways of thinking. How can we continue to be surprised when the cuts come, and ours are the first programs to go? I know the cuts have been harsh, but we are still in desperate need of innovation and new daring ways of caring. Perhaps, what I am proposing seems unrealistic in such hard fiscal times which force us into a kind of program anorexia – that is, our programs look lean and trim, but are fundamentally unhealthy and under-fed. However, changing our ways of thinking does not cost a penny. Besides, we need a change, and we need it now because regardless of the price of such a change, it will never cost us as much as the lives we are currently losing every day in America. We must take steps toward the unorthodox, and we must do so now.

Since orthodoxy has failed, and since without change, no change will occur, we must move toward more daring unorthodox programs. Remember that out on the limb is where the fruit grows – the fullest, ripest fruit, – but to reach it, we must totter and take a risk, every time. Ask any orchard owner, and he or she will tell you that fruit rarely grows in the safe places. Unorthodox thinking means that you hold a singular vision, which no one else has thought of or seen, and the programmatic expression of your vision will allow everyone to do what has not yet been done — reach the sweetest fruits. You often will find yourself out on a limb, reaching for that difficult-to-explain, difficult-to-grasp, newest, most daring idea. But, in the end, it is worth the risk of falling. After all, something brave must be undertaken, or else we will continue to count up our failures in the numbers of young people who we lose every day in America.

Regularly facing real-life circumstances is an enormous challenge, not to be taken lightly. Getting teens from where they are to where they want to be represents a quantum leap; we must realize that the journey starts with us. A simple change of attitude can be the beginning of lowering the national debt. When a teen looks in our eyes and sees his or her worth, the debt decreases immediately by one.

I

THE BEST CONTRACEPTIVE

As a long-time sexuality educator, I have tried (and regularly failed) to fashion educational techniques and approaches for teens in schools and community settings. I have tried to influence their thinking about delaying sexual intercourse during their adolescent years, or, at least, about using contraceptives conscientiously and consistently when choosing to have sex. I used information, current facts, frank discussions and fear-arousing techniques. I taught young women how to resist unwanted sexual advances. I sent males and females home with baby dolls that cried. I even had them carrying eggs around with them for days at a time. The groups I worked with met a variety of such guest lecturers as pregnant teenagers, teen fathers and mothers, adolescents with HIV, young people with STDs, teens with substance addictions, and young men and

I

women who had spent some time in jail. I took my students and young people from community programs to reproductive health clinics and foster homes. In an effort to use positive role-modeling, I brought in African-American, Asian-American, Latina, and Caucasian athletes, entertainment personalities, and other professionals to discuss their successes and their backgrounds. I think, in fact, I tried just about everything, whether in fashion or not, but mostly to no avail.

Looking back, I think that probably the single most meaningful thing I ever did to influence decision-making practices about pregnancy prevention was to bring in a 40 oz plastic soda container from the Seven-Eleven filled to the rim with sand from a local beach. I walked in the classroom, called the whole class up to the front table and dumped this giant cup of sand on it.

"Every time a male ejaculates," I said (or something to this effect), "this is the number of sperm which swim up the uterus after that one ovum, that one egg."

I stood there pointing at the sand, while they eyed the daunting pile of would-be sperm.

"There are no accidental pregnancies," I added for effect.

This simple, tangible, dramatic moment probably represents one of the few times that I have been able to be effective on the issue of teen pregnancy. Every teen, standing in front of that pile of sand, instantly and concretely understood the odds of pregnancy: millions of sperm swimming relentlessly toward a single ovum.

Perhaps the second most effective approach I

have used was to help young people see that they are worthwhile, capable of great achievements, able to accomplish wonderful things for themselves, their families, and communities. Impressing upon young people that they can set a course and reach whatever destination they choose has been effective. I have found, as I am sure many of you have learned, the most powerful contraceptive is activated when a young person believes he or she is a valuable individual who can and should make plans for a bright future; pregnancy is then viewed as a situation jeopardizing future plans. Hope for the future and an abiding faith that personal plans are worth protecting have the contraceptive effect of abstinence. Without a fundamental belief in the self, without faith in a positive future, any program we provide is stacked on an unsteady foundation; it will topple when faced with the first breeze of seduction or newly budding love.

We must help young people generate the belief that they are valuable individuals. We must help them locate and grasp a positive, hopeful outlook on their lives and their future. We must be like prospectors, helping them pan for the gold and treasures that exist within them. When you and the young people with whom you work get through the layers of resistance and doubt, of history and fear, when you locate their special talents and gifts, you will have tapped a source that will provide absolutely the best contraceptive.

I

IT'S ABOUT DESIRE

For the majority of my career educating young people (which began in 1959) I always had a vague feeling of discomfort about what I was able to truly accomplish. I always felt that, whether in schools or a community center, young people were close enough for me to touch, and yet still essentially out of my reach.

My response to this feeling was to try to improve my teaching and group techniques. I believed that if I somehow grew to be a more accomplished teacher, if I learned more, and accrued better interactive strategies, I would be able to reach them in a more satisfying way. If I could acquire a new approach, practice it, and deliver it *just so*, then, I thought, the disquieting feelings I had would disappear. Sometimes, I even resorted to blaming teens for my inability to reach them. At those moments, I thought they simply were not open to my approaches and entreaties. I believed, at times, that if they would only truly listen to me and try a little harder, then some of the information I was offering might make sense, and their lives would improve.

I was not fully aware of the fact that the young people who sat in those community centers and classrooms during those years had matters to focus on other than my messages, regardless of how well-developed and practiced my educational technique was. I was not aware that their concentration was taken up with more vital concerns, like whether an abusive parent would be home waiting for them, or whether food would be on the table for the next meal, or whether the electricity would be turned off because bills weren't being paid. There they were wondering if someone in the household finally got a job, and there I was trying to provide elegant learning activities, using the slickest, the latest, the most proven curriculum, wondering why they weren't responding to my bright approaches. There I was supplementing my work with compelling videos and flashy materials to improve their cognitive capacity. And there they were consumed with life-and-death matters, spending much of their youthful energy trying to survive another day, another week, trying to resolve very difficult, grown-up problems.

You can imagine my frustration, or maybe you know it by heart. I just could not understand why they did not see the concrete helpfulness of the most up-to-date decision-making models and sexual-responsibility principles I was providing. Why weren't they getting it? I thought: "Maybe it's me; no, it's probably them." Between blaming myself and them, I missed the true reason why nothing seemed to reach them: it was the environment of their lives which created barriers between us. In fact, what I was offering had no connection – none – to their reality. A superficial understanding about their real concerns and my all-absorbing drive to try out the latest methods and materials prevented me from reaching the core of their young, complex, troubled lives.

Talking with young people about safer sex or steps toward avoiding pregnancy could only have a limited impact upon adolescents concerned with living past their 18th birthday. Nonetheless, for years, I hammered away, trying to perfect my educational approach in order to resolve their problems. Since, at that time, my principal tool was a hammer, I naturally saw each of their problems as a nail; when I encountered barriers, I got myself more hammers.

Incidentally, my students liked me, gave excellent evaluations, and wanted to succeed the way I defined success. I wrote articles about them and even books explaining my approach, but all the while, very deep down, I knew that, in my work, I wasn't getting where I really wanted to go.

Then, after twenty-five years of such efforts, I was given a unique opportunity to add more tools to my repertoire of hammers. The Children's Aid Society provided me the chance to engage young people on the issues I had been trying to teach, but in a broader manner. I soon came to think of the problems facing teens as a construction site, and what I needed was a tool chest of saws, levels, screwdrivers, wrenches, and all of the necessary tools to engage teens and help them grow, especially those young people who intimately experienced suffering and despair. It was during this time that the vague gnawing discomfort I had experienced for so long began to be replaced by a sense of satisfaction and, once in a while, even jubilation, about the significant life-changes I could suddenly help young people make.

This shift occurred when I finally understood that simply providing adolescents with information, facts, data, and activities to increase their cognitive capacity was only the beginning of the work – the first stage, like drafting an architectural plan to a building – and not the end stage. I didn't need to give them more information, but instead I needed to help them develop the desire to achieve and maintain a safe, successful, healthy life.

Desire is the trigger that fires off healthy aspirations and actions. Desire produces abstinence and a delay in intercourse. Desire produces safer sexual behaviors. Desire produces conscientious contraceptive use. Desire produces impulse control. Desire reduces risk taking.

It's about desire because desire is the principal prerequisite for adolescents aiming to achieve their goals.

Each of us needs to reconceptualize our work, rethink our approaches, and candidly examine our professional practices to assess whether or not we are truly helping teens develop desire. Are we encouraging young people's desire to cultivate their gifts and talents, to utilize their strengths? It is a serious mistake to believe young people are ignorant and all we need to do to improve their lives is make them smart. Of course information and access are crucial to our efforts; however, we must link the facts with efforts to help them develop the will to have a successful life. We must not view teens as empty vessels into which we pour (or force) our wisdom. Our programs must be desire-based, not simply capacity-based, and certainly not fear-based. Desire-based programs champion a "Yes you can" view and help participants think and feel positively about the future. Desire-based programs create a climate of hopefulness, allowing everyone involved to believe that all things are possible. Desire-based programs emphasize the assets, achievements, and accomplishments of adolescents. Desire-based programs make it clear that no matter what a young person's past or present, no matter what they did or thought, they are safe with us and will have every single opportunity to succeed.

Desire-based programs make it clear to young people that through their participation, through their genuine efforts, employment will be within their reach; higher education and career or technical training will be a reality; primary health care will be an inalienable, protected right; and a non-judging, willing professional adult will always be there to help them through the inevitable valleys of despair which are associated with life.

This work of ours – it's about desire.

Life's mountain top work is helping

a young person have a better life.

———

Effective programs for young people and families

do not happen by spontaneous combustion;

someone must light a fire.

METAPHORS FOR WORKING WITH TEENS

II

II

LIFEGUARD WORK

Our efforts in working with teens equal that of a lifeguard. The lifeguard sits up high to get the best view of the potential danger zone. She is very focused and will not participate in distractions, since she knows that even the slightest straying of her eye can be fatal for those whose lives are entrusted to her. The lifeguard is trained to help. She is poised to help, and she will help, no matter the risk to herself.

Lifeguards who are focused and who pay attention usually make people feel secure to enter the water. The very presence of a watchful guard may even help people move into deeper waters where they can become better swimmers. Even when the water is over their heads, they will try because they know their lifeguard is focused and watchful, ready to help should something go wrong. Lifeguards actually provide people with an opportunity to be brave and succeed.

II

Suddenly (sometimes regularly), someone in the deep waters needs help. The person is panicking, thrashing about, afraid of drowning. In an instant, the lifeguard leaps from her perch and is on her way to help, as fast as she can, using all her energy to save this life. She does not stop along the way to seek permission from those sitting around. She is in the middle of an emergency; she is being called upon to save a life. She does not linger to engage in a conversation with on-lookers about the good old days when parents properly taught their children how to swim. She does not chat about how families today lack interest in teaching water skills.

No, this lifeguard does not have time to get permission to save a life or to stand around looking for family reasons to explain the current crisis. She understands that placing blame during an emergency only leads to greater suffering and a potential loss of life. No, placing blame never helps. Instead, she leaps into action, offering one-hundred-percent of herself. She is well aware of the risk to her life, but it does not stop her.

It is not uncommon for a drowning person to surrender to panic and terror and to actually fight the lifeguard who is trying to help. In fact, sometimes, a person in such a dangerous situation will resist powerfully and fiercely, fighting off every attempt to be rescued. Lifeguards are not surprised by this response; they are ready to counter resistance and will do anything to save a life.

One thing a lifeguard never does is swim away from a drowning person, especially when the victim is resisting help. A lifeguard never treads water at a safe distance and yells out that she will

II

provide help only when proper motivation and compliance are demonstrated. The lifeguard never says, "Well, obviously you are not ready for my help. Take a little time now and think about that; when you're ready to be saved, give me a signal by raising your hand, and I will rescue you."

No, genuine lifeguards have no requirements to be met before they will help. In fact, their own desire to save the person energizes them to fight through resistance, to risk their own lives, and do what is necessary to get the job done. Sometimes, this means subduing the drowning person and taking them safely to shore.

Your work is nothing less than that of a lifeguard. Be prepared and ever watchful. Expect resistance, subdue if necessary, but never swim away.

II

II

THE RAGING RIVER

Many professionals working with young people have become frustrated and exhausted in their efforts to keep pace with the mounting tragedies affecting teens today. It is not unusual for youth workers to feel that working with teens is like facing a raging river into which many young people have fallen. In great numbers, teens are being carried down stream by a dangerous current; since they have not been taught skills to negotiate the swift rapids or to keep their heads above water, many young people are being swept under.

In order to deal with such a crisis, the worker must leap into the treacherous current. With an expenditure of enormous energy and by extraordinary effort, he or she is sometimes able to drag a young person to the safety of the river bank. Saving just one young person all but drains the worker.

II

Suddenly, however, there is a panicked shout for help, as another young person is caught in the swirling current, almost out of reach. With great resolve but little reserve, the worker leaps in and is able to save this second young person.

As these events are unfolding, it becomes clear to the worker that many young people are being dragged downstream by the current. Some are in plain view, but others have drown, already swept out of sight. Many are crashing against the rocky shores and ledges of the river, broken and beyond help. Other workers arrive and begin wading into the stream, rescuing young people, while the first worker regains strength. It is clear to everyone that more and more young people are falling in, bobbing in dangerous waters, and drowning. There are not enough workers to retrieve and resuscitate. Such odds produce exhaustion, little respite, and few successes. Our daunting reality is that few are saved by our efforts; many are lost.

Working in adolescent prevention and service programs on issues like pregnancy, HIV, substance abuse, violence, homophobia, and STDs, we often face the raging river and the haunting, hopeless feelings that we are losing, not winning, in our efforts to save teens. Lately, in order to reach more young people, we have had to redouble our efforts with yet scarcer resources.

Changing our focus marks the beginning of wisdom in recognizing what is truly needed in such trying times. While continuing the short-term emergency triage and resuscitation, we must lift our sights upstream to locate the reason for these tragedies. Where are these young people coming from? How are they winding up in such a life-threatening situation?

Upstream, not surprisingly, we easily locate the problem: a pathway over this dangerous river has crumbled. Gaps and rusted steel leave huge cavities in the bridge's structure where it crosses the most dangerous waters. Some young people seem to know instinctively to be cautious; others are strong enough to climb through the dangerous areas, but many blindly approach and, finding themselves unable to hold on, suddenly drop right through the open crevices, falling to the swift current below where they are propelled into the flow.

What needs to be done is obvious: it is time to repair that dangerous bridge. The damage to the infrastructure is so extensive that it may require fundamental structural work, and it may take a very long time to make a safe passage, but nonetheless, the patience to rebuild and an investment of resources to get the job done are crucial. Some will say there isn't time for a fundamental restructuring of the foundation; others will say the price is too high for us to attempt to rebuild the bridge. They will propose using temporary filler, building right on top of that unstable structure in order to cut costs. But such attempts will easily come undone, as they have only the appearance of being safe. The weight of so many young people is considerable; teens are counting on us to provide a sturdy and dependable way to cross the river because they need a safe passage.

Attempts to frighten young people into being careful as they cross the gaping path or to sanction them with even greater punishment if they should

II

slip and fall, are all misguided. Punishment and rhetorical political slogans are no substitute for truly solving the problem. We do not need to give our young people training in obstacle course completion; we need to create a safe path for them.

Our labor therefore must be focused on creating a secure journey; we must repair the bridge.

II

II

II

STARFISH

While our work in sexuality, sexual orientation, HIV, substance abuse, violence, STDs, pregnancy prevention, and all the other adolescent challenges may seem staggering, it is crucial for us to keep our eye on the ball. While the number of young people in our programs are at times unmanageable — sometimes even interfering with our ability to provide help — while the situation is often so frustrating that it drains our energy, we must remember that one, three, or five young people may silently benefit because of our efforts.

Imagine that because of your work a few people find a better path, improve their lives and become more productive for themselves, their families, their communities. What a justification for your time on earth! What a great deed it is to have been an instrument of fundamental change.

If every worker provided the support and aid for just one young person to create a better life, we would have a momentous movement on our hands.

And it all will have begun by helping just one.

A fairly well-known story told among youth workers illustrates the point: early one morning, on a long beach, an adult decided to go for a walk and came across a young woman, throwing something into the sea.

"What are you doing?" he asked.

"Pretty soon," she explained, "the sun is going to come out and dry up all these starfish, so I am throwing them back before they die."

"But there are millions," the man pointed out. "What difference do you think you can really make?"

The young woman considered his question for a moment, and surveyed the long expanse of the beach, which was indeed filled with starfish washed up on the shore.

She bent down and picked up a starfish, resuming her efforts.

"Well," she said, finally answering, "I'll make a difference to this one."

And with that, she tossed the starfish into the sea.

Make a difference to one.

II

II

TUGBOAT, SAILBOAT, RAFT

When working with young people, what kind of a vessel are you?

Are you a tugboat? A tugboat fights the currents, rides the swells and dips into deep waters, but always reappears to pull ahead. A tugboat can handle weights much greater than its own. It attaches itself to the struggling and the stalled, offering up its own energy to make the voyage. Sometimes, a tugboat is called in to save huge ships and cargoes that have run into trouble. It must right these vessels, trudge through great turbulence, dragging them to a safer place where they can be fixed. The tugboat is solid, dependable, has great endurance, and can be counted on to provide a safe passage. When the tugboat arrives on the scene, all spirits are lifted or buoyed, for problems will soon be overcome. It may be unglamorous to be a tugboat. It may be

II

uncelebrated, but a sturdy force is always called upon as a guide in times of trouble; there are many sinking and in need of a pull.

Are you a sailboat? The sailboat needs wind to move. In fact, without the right conditions, the sailboat sits without movement, looking great, but going nowhere. With the wind, when the weather is perfect, the colorful sails unfurl, and swift beautiful movement is created. But everything that the sailboat does depends on external elements. Think about it, are you a sailboat? Are you at your best only when there are outside forces moving you?

Or perhaps you're a raft: a raft goes with the current, and is not able to move on its own. It bounces around with prevailing forces and cannot set or correct its own course. For a raft, there is no captain, no charted course. Rafts cannot offer help;

they are working under the fear of being capsized or swamped. Their speed depends on the fickleness of the wind and the current.

What kind of worker are you?

What kind will you become?

II

II

THE VINEYARD: A PARABLE FOR OUR WORK AND TIMES

There is a scriptural passage about a vineyard owner who is not happy with the growth and yield of a fruit-bearing tree in his vineyard. He tells a worker to cut the tree down and plant another in its place. The vineyard worker speaks up, asking the owner to give him more time with the tree, to give this tree another chance. The worker promises to re-nourish the soil, to water it more than usual, to clear away the other branches and make sure it receives the proper sunlight.

"And then perhaps next season, this tree will bear us fruit," the worker says.

The owner agrees, and the worker, keeping up his part of the bargain, is diligent and resolute in the task. Within a year, the fruit-bearing tree that once was almost fire-wood is part of the glory of the orchard, bearing more fruit than the worker can pick.

This is a helpful parable for our work: just like the tree, many of the young people in our daily work need more time, more attention, and more care. They need us to have faith that with our careful attention they will bear fruit. They need us to remain loyal in barren times. They need to know our solution is not to simply get rid of them, or replace them, or expend our concentrated efforts only on those who are more open to us, those who are more productive, those who already bear fruit. Instead of these tactics, we must try again and again and again to stimulate growth, to nourish the soil with encouragement, to pull back the branches that shield the sun. The buds are there; the fruit will grow with our help. Young people need direct sunlight, warmth, and our full attention in order to flourish.

A few teens in your work may have received these essentials in their lives; they may need less attention. Others, having long been deprived, will need to be heated directly with warming rays of gentleness, generosity, and encouragement. Be mindful of this vineyard worker: he was willing to take the extra steps to ensure that fruit would grow, though it meant having patience and waiting another season for the yield.

All of the young people in our work deserve repeated chances to grow and bear fruit. We must be patient and positive, like the vineyard worker, who was willing to feed, safeguard, and nourish his tree. No matter how barren the young people, or how hopeless the task may seem, we can provide the right circumstances for teens to grow. It is helpful to remember that a great many successes began as impossible tasks. Remember, too, that the next good deed we do for a young person may be the time the miracle of growth occurs.

II

II

BE A FLARE – BE INCENDIARY!

If you have changed the path, or readied the road, or lit the sky for a mere instant to provide a clear vision for a single young person whose life would otherwise be in darkness, then you have justified your life's work.

As youth workers, teachers, counselors, and ministers, we face enormous tasks and great burdens that often produce significant frustrations and palpable feelings of failure. These feelings are a given in our work; still, we must never surrender or add our own hopelessness to that of struggling teens. We are the ones in the equation who must be hopeful. We must be so hopeful and have such a repertoire upon which to call that we can literally grasp hold of these young people and lift them up to a new place.

We can help them develop roots to grow and wings to fly. Such extraordinary events can occur; I

II

have witnessed them, and I believe you have too.

Believe that you are important, that you are meaningful. Believe that you can make a difference. You must be willing and able to do anything to make a difference. Such a conviction and your palpable belief in young people will be more powerful than any piece of information, book, or video.

Illuminate the path for young people.

A flare creates a light that's brighter than light. You must be a flare so that they will see their path very clearly and will know that along the way someone will be there, even when things go bad, as they inevitably will. It will be okay when things go wrong because you will not turn away in times of trouble.

In the lives of many of these young people, important adults have always disappeared. But this time, someone will accompany them as they move through the valleys of their development and reach the mountain top of their potential. This time, the adult will not disappear, but instead will light up the sky, making it daylight and bringing clarity.

Effective individual and team efforts with young people will not happen by spontaneous combustion. You (or your organization) cannot become a flare, a bright light, a bonfire, unless someone first strikes a match. Now is the time for you to be incendiary in your efforts.

II

Young people frequently forget what we say and do,

but they rarely forget how we make them feel.

———

Our job is to find the gift in each young person –

Keep looking!

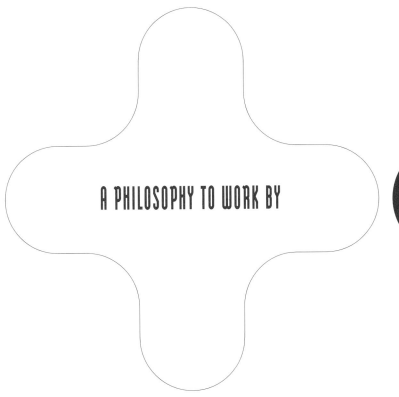

A PHILOSOPHY TO WORK BY

III

III

ADOLESCENT SEXUALITY: LOOKING ABOVE THE WAIST

For the majority of parents, school policy-makers, and government officials, the phrases "family life," "sex education," and "human sexuality" are simply code words for school programs discussing sex acts, contraception, and safer sex techniques. Many believe that these words camouflage instructions on who does what to whom, in what position, how many times, and how to avoid undesirable outcomes while "doing it." In many communities, sexuality education has come to mean explanations of below-the-waist genital acts. Therefore, the primary challenge for those working in sexuality with teens is to communicate a holistic, above-the-waist definition of sexuality and sexual expression.

While issues of genital-sexual behaviors and their potential outcomes are critical to explore with young people, an obsession about adolescent inter-

III

course continues to dominate our work. These efforts have created an overwhelmingly genital focus and an all around unhealthy environment for discussing sexuality with young people. We wrongly portray sexuality as an event. And what a profound disservice this is to teens because it narrows and distorts their understanding of themselves. In the meantime, we continue to reduce sexuality education to discussions about disease, life-and-death, and a burdened and compromised future. By arousing their fear, we engage in a process to terrify them about sexuality and its many expressions.

Adolescent sexuality is not an activity; it is not an event; it is not a behavior. Instead, adolescent sexuality is an extensive, complex, and potentially joyful area of life. It is spiritual, intellectual, emotional, religious, and cultural, as well as biological.

Discussions of "sexual activity" should not merely include only intercourse and contraception. Adolescent sexual activity includes kissing, flirting, touching, holding, hugging, fantasy, sensuality, and erotic behaviors.

By spending so much time in schools and community agencies on relentless discussions about genital sexual behaviors; by saturating teens with videos about abstinence, safer sex, and contraception, we have in effect performed a *sexectomy* on our young people. We have separated sex from the rest of life. We have divided and compartmentalized the genitals from the whole person. We have reduced an essential and fulfilling life force by describing it *in genitalia* only, which we then deny.

I believe that we need to stop looking below the waist. I believe we need to raise our sights and

III

look to the full person. This task represents the principal challenge in the sexuality field today. I believe that raising our sights will signify a quantum leap from a narrow focus on sex acts, behaviors, and genitals to a more holistic, organic view of sexuality and sexual expression. Of course, such a leap will be difficult, since many of the influences that shape sexuality (Hollywood, the media, television) relay messages that are superficial, cosmetic, and slick. These powerful factors reinforce the genital focus which we have all been taught to believe constitute our essential sexual nature.

A holistic grasp of sexuality redefines it as an essential life force, both organic and inherent to the total person. The holistic philosophy maintains that sexuality is expressed in a variety of ways, not singularly through our genitals alone, whether by ourselves or with a partner.

Sexuality is expressed through our social, gender, and family roles. It is expressed through non-genital means of affection, love, and intimacy. It is expressed erotically, sensually, and, yes, genitally. However, genital sexual expression is only one fiber of the total fabric, and one fiber does not constitute the whole cloth. Many, many fibers woven together in unique patterns constitute the whole cloth that is a person's sexuality.

Thus through lectures, discussion groups, and videos, we must emphasize that genital-sexual behavior is only one aspect of sexuality, and that there is a great capacity for varied sexual expression. If we must obsess, let it be about body image, gender roles, social and family roles, sensuality, and the vast ways of showing affection, love, and inti-

III

macy. These fundamental elements constitute the whole person; they are the woven fibers creating each person's sexual potential.

Our sexuality lessons must explore above-the-waist issues like the impact and role of gender. Many young people are excited by opportunities to gain genuine insight into this complex dimension. However, society tends to eroticize all relationships between men and women and to objectify and depersonalize the gendered aspects of the individual. These elements continue to influence teens, who are very interested in trying to discern what it means to be male and what it means to be female. Socialization remains strongly gender-specific and, at times, limiting. Strong social factors create segregated male psyches and female psyches, which can make our work challenging, to say the least. For

III

these reasons, gender-role exploration should constitute a major thrust in all sexuality education.

Another dimension of adolescent sexuality, which needs our attention, is body image, or how young people feel and perceive themselves and how they perceive others. Confidence and feelings of security about the "rightness" of one's body can facilitate healthy expressions of sexuality. Conversely, doubt and anxiety about one's body can inhibit healthy sexual expression. For example, adolescent males have received the message, loudly and clearly, that they should do and not feel. Their masculinity rests on a strong body that is able to perform. Adolescent females learn that "looks count." All of their biological changes during puberty are monitored and interpreted through a filter of the ideal cultural appearance. Young women quickly

III

learn to view their bodies cosmetically and superficially; they are socialized to use these standards and look to others for validation of their femininity.

An adolescent concept of self is greatly influenced and powerfully affected by gender socialization, by lessons in closeness, caring and tenderness toward people of both sexes, and by values within a familial and societal context. Only recently have we begun to pay attention to the struggle of males and females of all ages to control their deepest feelings lest they be labeled "inappropriate" to their sex. If we want future generations of adults to interact with others in secure, intimate, loving ways, then the sexual learning of adolescents must include an exploration of feelings, affection, and intimacy in the context of gender expectations and in the context of simply being a human being.

III

III

EVERY YOUNG PERSON IS PURE POTENTIAL

Many of the young people we see in our community agencies, institutions, and schools carry around deep, but active, feelings of helplessness, hopelessness, guilt, and shame. We may never personally feel the direct expression of these forces, but every day we can observe their behavioral results. Hostility, for instance, irresponsible actions, attitudes of indifference, and many postures are expressions of deeply held pain. Young people have learned to cover over their anguish, to put up fronts, to seek out anesthesia to dull difficult emotions and take the edge off.

Unfortunately, rather than recognizing the origin of these challenging and sometimes insulting behaviors, we often simply react to them, trying to retaliate with control, power, and insistence on conformity. In the end, we make things worse by engaging in the conflict. Instead we must understand that

III

what drives the frustrating teen behavior is not a personal vendetta against us. Never having been taught to acknowledge or understand their behaviors, teens tend to express them in unconscious ways that create barriers or cause trouble.

Having worked with teens for almost four decades, I know that the best way to transcend these complex problems is to look at every young person as absolutely pure potential. I believe that we must view every young person individually as someone with great gifts, talents, and assets. Our role is to help young people find and double their treasures. I have found that by acting on such a belief, I am able to look past the posturing and unhelpful attitudes, the fearful testing of power, and the puffing of a chest which dares me to care; I have learned to take a much deeper, truer view of the young person in front of me.

III

Whenever we treat teens as if they are an accident about to happen, whenever we try to mind-read them or act as if they are bound to disappoint, we all but ensure a tense, unfriendly, empty relationship that will quickly be over. Remember, these young people are not disposable, they are not statistical cattle. They are not the percentage of young women who become pregnant, or the future suicides of our nation. They are not the young men who become fathers by the age of fifteen, or the gun-carrying marauders you hear about on the news. They are, instead, future successes waiting to happen, human beings waiting for someone to believe in them.

Put aside traditional views and replace them with a belief in the goodness of the young person. You will notice the difference in your work immediately, and you will feel so good.

III

SELF – ESTEEM: CAUGHT NOT TAUGHT

Self-esteem is a tremendously critical issue in the lives of all people, especially in the lives of those with whom we work. Lately, however, there seems to be a movement based on the idea that self-esteem can be taught, that all we need to do is "teach it" with the proper video, workbooks, or curricula, which, we are told, are easy to purchase and use. I believe this is a dangerous idea. Self-esteem is caught not taught. Within the context of a school or community program, helping teens feel better about themselves requires realizing that you must make a great investment of time and energy: this is what it takes to enhance a young person's self-esteem.

III

From the moment a child leaves the secure, spiritual environment of the mother's womb and enters the social environment of life, he or she is usually held and nurtured by an adult, often a mother or father, sometimes a grandparent, foster parent, or another adult nurturer. The lavishing of affection that begins at this time is equivalent to creating an endowment of affection; essentially, such affection begins the development of a young person's self-esteem endowment.

During the early phase of a child's life, adults provide looks, touches, and words of love in order to communicate that the infant is a valued person and family member. The infant needs such affection to grow, as any living being needs food or oxygen.

In some families, money is saved for an infant's future education and financial needs; similarly, a self-esteem endowment is created with love and affection so that the child will be able to meet emotional needs throughout his or her life.

Infants have incredibly precise antennae for

loving expressions; they seek out affection and absorb it hungrily, and store it – so grows the endowment. Adults play a crucial role in this equation: they are loving teachers and teachers of love. Loving is learned during this early period and forms the fundamental infrastructure of the infant's capacity for affection. Loving words, phrases, and touches are actually the principal funds invested, forming the infant's self-esteem endowment.

III

"You're so beautiful," a father says to his son.

"You're a very smart little girl," a grandmother says to her granddaughter.

"I can't wait to hold you in my arms," a mother tells her child.

These sentiments represent deposits in the self-esteem bank and grow to make the endowment.

Throughout the years, more is added, and, in

fact, it is critical that a steady affectionate and loving stream of deposits continues; the interest from this endowment will later provide confidence and stability to produce healthy behaviors. In this way, an infant moves through childhood into adolescence, becoming a young person who will be able to behave in ways that are responsible, rather than exploitive or self-destructive. The extent to which this endowment grows and becomes secure will predict the extent to which this young person will be able to avoid harmful behaviors. In fact, the interest generated from this account drives the child's behavior, his or her very actions and attitudes.

A young person whose self-esteem endowment is substantial will have such a self-confidence income that he or she will never be overdrawn no matter what the demand.

Accordingly, we must keep in mind that many of the young people we work with in community agencies, in institutions, and schools, are often lacking a substantial self-esteem endowment. For one or another reason, they did not receive the income of adult words of support, encouragement, affection, and generosity. This inadequate legacy did not prepare them with feelings of self-worth and confidence, so that they could face the world without a crippling fear or sense of deprivation. As a result, these youngsters are very fragile, and no amount of short-term teaching, workshop or talent assessments will help, "increase their self-esteem," as popular terminology has it.

Low self-esteem is probably the single most critical challenge when working with youth; it has a crippling effect. The challenge is difficult, since we

III

III

cannot just start back at the beginning and provide a historically proper endowment of love, affection, generosity, gentleness, and caring. Neither can we simply provide some information about their talents and possibilities, hoping it's sufficient to ensure their success and happiness. No, our task is a complicated process, especially when we remember that many of the young people in our work have suffered for many years. Accordingly, our initial task in this remedial process is to work with the young person to deconstruct, or break down, all the negative constructs that have been built: the unhelpful attitudes, information, beliefs, and resulting actions employed over the years to compensate for the insufficient self-esteem endowment.

Being mindful of the investment needed, we must work slowly and consciously with the young person to deconstruct existing unhealthy and unhelpful information and attitudes which have been absorbed in earlier years. Notions we will need to address over a long period of time include: "Failing only a couple of subjects isn't too bad"; "A little force to get what you want is okay"; "It is okay to use sex to get what you want or need"; "If someone bothers you, then pound them; that'll teach them not to mess with you." We must not subsidize these messages in any way; nothing makes them right. You know that young people are capable of so much more, and it is your job to demonstrate your belief in their ability to change and grow.

All through the deconstruction process, it is important to keep in mind that unhealthy behaviors and attitudes are usually coping mechanisms which have outlasted their usefulness. Therefore, they must

III

be replaced by something concrete, rather than something rhetorical or pat. This kind of healing and developing of new coping and life skills takes time. What follows deconstruction is the even harder job of setting the stage for a new kind of future.

After deconstruction, much healing will be needed. Reparations and preparations for new healthy growth always take time. Helping young people develop faith and healthy strategies for tackling life's difficulties is a long, incredible journey. Supporting teens as they learn to master new skills and providing them opportunities to become competent are essential elements in creating an abundant self-esteem endowment. All along the way, self-esteem enhancement must be encouraged by showing the young person that you believe in him or her, by offering praise and gentleness, by being honest,

III

caring, and faithful. This is the beginning of asset accumulation in developing the crucial self-esteem endowment.

The point is this: remedial self-esteem work is labor-intensive; it requires a full understanding of a how a person develops a sense of personality, identity, and character. You can become the main depositor in the self-esteem endowment of each young person. Your work can contribute to the increase and growth of that intangible, emotional sum that will become a positive force in that young person's life and will yield significant, positive behavioral interest.

In our work, with this new view, we can become professionals who deposit self-esteem. The attitude we take should be that no matter what the nature of our interaction with a young person, we

III

want to somehow add to the endowment.

We fail in our work when we make a with-drawal, raid their accounts by our actions, or have them pay a penalty for short-comings, whether ours or theirs. We must be brave, face our mistakes, and never make a withdrawal. We must make the invest-ment and contribute as often as possible.

Remember: every penny counts.

III

III

III

SOME THOUGHTS ON MOTIVATION

Among the litany of complaints about young people today is their alleged lack of motivation. This criticism comes from government officials, public policy makers, teachers, counselors, and youth workers. The implication of the underlying accusation is clear: young people just don't want to help themselves (the way we did); they don't have the drive, the dedication, or the energy to succeed (the way we did). I have heard people say, "How come more young people today are not passionate about improving themselves? In my day, I took any job and did anything to improve my situation!"

Some people even go so far as to believe that all young people really need is a good old fashion talking-to, which will threaten them into motivation or punish them into dedication. I wouldn't be at all surprised if someone is, at this moment, developing

III

a surefire curriculum, an educational inoculation, which will inject the proper dosage of motivation into young people, infuse just the right amount of drive. I wouldn't be surprised if someone has already patented a Norplant-like device which will ooze a five-year dose of ambition directly into the bloodstream of young people. A plan to obliterate alleged adolescent arrogance, apathy, and indifference is probably just on the horizon. Sayings like, "It's motivation, stupid," will become chic.

But, seriously, motivation is not something that is controlled by the individual, simply turned on and off. A drive toward personal achievement, improvement, and success, motivation comes from within. A motivated teen has a vision, a direction, and a font of energy applied toward realizing that dream. Motivation helps him or her overcome all barriers, fight through resistance and doubt, and maintain a focus on the goal. These elements cannot be instantly cultivated in a person who has suffered.

As we all know, family problems often produce children with problems. Problems dilute motivation. Emotional and physical pain impedes or slows the genesis of motivation, while suffering prevents the conversion of any existing motivation into action. Young people who have been wounded during their early development generally have a difficult time demonstrating the kind of motivation that adults love to see because the spark required to ignite motivation has been dampened. The much-needed spark, in fact, is continually exposed to the moisture left over from early damage, preventing it from ever lighting a fire.

Fear of the future and fear in the present

obstruct motivation. Fear is a main component of life for many young people, a reality that impedes the development and expression of the kind of energy ensuring genuine motivation and ambition.

Humiliation cripples motivation. Humiliation about education, family relationships, housing, unemployment, and economic status cripples motivation and makes it next to impossible to carry out motivated behaviors and to achieve our program goals. Fear and humiliation numb all the senses and drain energy sources. Fear and humiliation are tremendous burdens.

However, once a few of those burdens are lifted and some of those wounds of humiliation and fear begin to heal, motivation bubbles up. I have witnessed this myself in numerous young people who have seen life become less harsh, who have had chaos replaced by order. When their hurt and shame begin to heal, young people have a great capacity for resilience and growth. Recuperation and restoration stimulate positive feelings about the self and frequently yield desirable qualities associated with aspiration and achievement. In my many years of working with young people and their families, I have seen that after having their basic needs fulfilled, teens can make a quantum leap toward motivated behaviors.

A starting place in this process is communicating that young people are good and worthwhile. They need to hear that their bodies are clean, their ideas are valuable: they are capable of living responsible, moral lives, capable of great things. These assertions are an important part of the services we provide. Our belief in their worth will help kindle

III

in them a belief in themselves. Young people have so
few guides in the shrinking world of youth services.
We must be their guides, filling ourselves and them
with patience and respect, and we must do so without paternalism. These are the elements that constitute a successful paradigm, making it possible for
that inherent motivation in young people to bubble
up to the surface of their lives.

III

III

III

THIS IS A TEST

1) *The most important element in working with young people is (circle only one response):*

    A) the worker;

    B) the agency policy;

    C) the curriculum or philosophy behind the work;

    D) the young person;

III

It is healthy to view a young person as the most important element in teaching, counseling, advocacy, and service provision. This means that the teens we see are more essential than the material we use, than our agency's or school's reputation, than our own status or personal beliefs. The elevation of young people to the primary position of importance communicates a genuine message of caring to them and positively effects the whole workplace. The way for this elevation to occur is relatively simple: we must value them above everything else.

Young people must know you regard them as significant individuals. Of course this does not ensure that at first they won't be skeptical; remember, many young people have had a lifetime of experiences contrary to the ones they will experience with you. They may not be used to a caring, generous, gentle adult who honestly regards them as the most important person in each exchange.

Remember too that while the young person is central in your work, without you nothing happens, just as without the vineyard worker no flowers bloom, no trees bear fruit. You are the catalyst, the "miracle grow," the leaven that rises the dough. You are the one who can see the treasure deep inside each one of them. You are the one who communicates through feeling, attitude, and action that they are special. When you do this on a daily basis in your work, it shows; it elevates the interaction to a new, very special plane. Oh what joy there is in knowing that you are no longer missing the mark! The feeling is indescribable.

I know this goal is not easy to accomplish, but there comes a point in our work-life, when a new kind of creativity must take hold in us if we truly care and want to change and improve ourselves in order to change and improve others. We know we have reached this point when we change our prophesy about young people. We know we have reached this point when our attitudes change.

Because we care so much and are desperate to help teens, we will be able to lift them to a place of importance in our work, in our organization, and in our hearts.

III

III

EMOTIONAL INCOME: OUR FAT PAYCHECK

The principal income we derive from working with young people cannot be spent in stores and cannot be used to pay our bills or family expenses. While we are paid in American dollars, we know our principal income is emotional. Sometimes the emotional income from helping young people grow is immense: good feelings course through our blood stream, affecting every cell in our body, generating and renewing, filling us with clarity and passion. This is a natural high that no chemicals can match; perhaps it is the very experience that keeps us coming back to face the complex and painful problems of working with teens.

The work we put out in order to get such a meaningful emotional salary is great. Physically, it is time-consuming and exhausting; sometimes, it feels as if every day is Monday. Evenings and weekends

III

are frequently spent working or thinking about work. Finding time for family and friends becomes a challenge which sometimes strains those important supports and relationships in our lives. While the highs are high, the lows are often very low, and working in the valleys for long periods of time, quickly depletes the emotional income, reduces resiliency, and affects judgment. This is the hard reality of working with young people.

Must we be reminded just how needed we are? Family systems have gotten weaker. The fragmentation of society prevents young people from developing secure resources or an accurate picture of their own strengths. Young people, today, in fact, are suffering more and growing up with more deficits. How often have we run across a young person who has received so little in life that we are left thinking, "Who raised this child?" or "My God, how could this have happened?" Sometimes we wish we could take a young person's life and start it all over again. But we cannot. The deficits along every measure of healthy and normal development are great. Desperate family and community histories often predict hopelessness, futility, and fatalism. This does not mean, however, that our efforts are ineffective. It means, we better roll up our sleeves because there's no time to waste, and there's a lot to be done.

Young people have enormous resilience. They are extremely capable of bouncing back and overcoming what appears to be insurmountable odds. They often are miraculously able to overcome great adversity, especially when there is a generous and steady adult around to guide the way. Young people

III

in the most desperate of circumstances are capable of quantum gains when someone genuinely cares, offers patience, and endures.

Your work is demanding.

Collect that emotional paycheck whenever you can; it is earned income.

III

III

Never taking a risk with a young person is

the biggest risk of all.

Do not underestimate the power of genuinely caring.

NEW VISION: ATTITUDES AND PRACTICES

IV

CARING: A PRACTITIONER'S PRIMER

Genuine caring is the context within which all help occurs. There are no degrees, no training, and workshops when it comes to caring: you either care or you don't. Caring is not a matter of partial effort or second best. The kind of care we must offer to young people in our schools or institutions is not ambivalent, apathetic, or indifferent. Practitioners of care are fully present. They truly listen and truly communicate, a word derived from the Latin *communis*, meaning to have something in common.

Practitioners of care understand pain and suffering, and, in some cases, may even share such pain. They understand that their caring soothes, and gentleness and tenderness are like balms that heal wounds. Practitioners of care are liberated from their own burdening need to control and calculate. Perhaps the reason that traditional, quick-fix solu-

IV

tions have failed is this lack of commitment to care. Caring is our human capital: a currency bubbling up from within, a well-spring fed by our spirit and breath. Caring is a deep desire, a passion to provide valuable services to young people independent of governmental largesse, foundation priorities, or donor commitments. Caring cannot be downsized or cut.

When others say, "Hey, look, I don't care. It's your life; go ahead and do what you want. I get paid either way," the gentle practitioner says: "Let's figure this out together. I care about what happens to you. I do not want to see you get hurt anymore. I want to understand and help if I can."

The core of really caring is when you do not know what to do, when you do not know how to soothe or cure, when you face the powerlessness of working with teens, but do not let these feelings stop you. Often, it is at these very standstill moments that opportunities for the most caring and healing arise.

The practitioner of care knows about such moments and is willing to offer his or her services, no matter the final outcome. The practitioner of care understands that some young people will continue down a path of suffering, unable to accept genuine offers of help, but also that the offering itself will make a difference somewhere on that road.

IV

IV

THE PARALLEL FAMILY – SYSTEMS APPROACH

Adopting a parallel family-systems approach is necessary to change our failing philosophy behind working with teens in the areas of sexuality, drugs, violence, and HIV. The approach dictates that we simply treat each young person as if he or she were our own child. Not looking to supplant already existing family networks, we are merely providing additional support for young people who are struggling to make their way through adolescence.

The parallel family-systems approach cuts right to the core of the issue by requiring youth workers to ask the following in every situation: "If this were my son or daughter, what would I want to happen? What would I want this young person to know, to do, to believe, or to feel? How can I ensure safety for this young person? Where do I want this teen to go in life; where does he or she want to go?

IV

What kind of person can I help him or her be?"
When we ask ourselves these questions concerning
our own family members, we usually come up with
very concrete answers and actions. The same should
be true for the young people with whom we work.

IV

If we accept this approach, our overall work
habits will change dramatically. We will not allow
teens to leave our offices, classrooms, counseling
sessions without the benefit of our absolute best
efforts. We will not leave irresponsible views
unchallenged. We will use all of our creative thinking, resources, and advocacy skills to advance the
potential for success in each young person. Using a
parallel family-systems approach will provide you
with a new perspective, similar to the one that drove
you to work with young people in the first place; it
will create increased passion and energy in you.

This approach requires a whole new attitude for engaging and working with teens; it requires a context of genuine care. The parallel family-systems approach must be integrated into your deepest beliefs; it must be used consistently. You cannot simply memorize this point-of-view, since memorizing is not understanding. In fact, memorization is superficial and quickly disappears.

IV

We must adopt attitudes similar to those we accept in our own nuclear and extended families in our roles as parents, caretakers, and adults. Patience is one such attribute, which, like a rope, allows us to continue our upward climb with young people, despite the height of the mountain, despite inevitable setbacks, resistance, and difficult challenges. Having patience often means beginning again and again with optimism and enthusiasm; it means not backing down or giving up in the face of stubbornness or even defeat.

With patience, cheerfulness surmounts despair.

With patience, hopefulness conquers fatalism.

Youth workers, teachers, and counselors must have realistic expectations regarding the possible outcomes of their interventions with each unique, struggling young person. In some circumstances, very modest outcomes can be achieved to help develop a solid foundation for work later on. In other situations, the worker or teacher will have more time with the teen, resulting in more ambitious work and greater outcomes.

There is a very accurate, popular saying lately that it takes a whole village to raise a child. However, it also takes an enormous amount of time to raise that child – days, weeks, months, and years of work must be given by committed adults in order for a young person to move from hopelessness to industriousness and optimism. There are no short-cuts, no special curricula, no quick fixes or government appropriations to help guide young people on their journey; there is only us. The solution seems old fashioned in such high-tech times: putting in a full day's work behind the plow, digging deep, pushing through resistance, and returning each dawn to continue the work until it's time to reap a harvest.

Using the parallel family-systems approach does not suggest that we have no limits or standards by which to guide our work with young people. Just as in families where certain expectations regarding decorum and respect are firmly in place and understood, we should set those rules in our work, as well. Remember, though, limits and standards without compassion are mere power plays on our part.

Approach young people, then, with a kind of firm warmth ("firmth" if you will). If your interaction or teaching style is characterized by gentleness and caring along with passion and a firm expression of your expectations, then your efforts will be meaningful in the lives of many, many adolescents.

IV

IV

SOME BASIC TOOLS

Over the years, while teaching and training, I have often been asked which strategies, interventions, and approaches have been most effective in achieving the best outcomes for adolescents. The answer is this: there is no single approach for working with teens that in itself has been successful. However, what has been effective in my work is a combination of gentleness, patience, generosity, faith, and forgiveness. I consider these the essential tools of our trade, essential to success in any helping field. This is not to say that I have always understood what was needed and when to use it; in fact, I've had to teach myself how to become an affectionately active worker.

What I've learned while working with teens for so many years is to be creative and prepared for the unexpected. Their problems are varied and complex, often unpredictable: we need an entire tool

IV

chest with us at all times, since it is difficult to predict what problem we will face and what tool we will
need.

When working with teens, I consider the
following tools essential:

Gentleness: means never threatening or challenging
young people in order to establish authority, structure, or control. In our work, gentleness means genuinely listening and fully attending to each young
person who speaks and somehow demonstrates that
he or she needs attention. In our work, gentleness
means never humiliating a young person to make
others laugh, or to keep them in their place, or to
save face, or to appear to be in control. Gentleness
means creating an environment where thoughts and
feelings are respected and never taken for granted.

Generosity: means always interpreting the best of intentions in the behaviors of teens. When problems occur, as they regularly do, generosity means we will work through issues, not hold grudges, and be interested in moving on when things are thoroughly resolved. In our work, generosity means never seeking retaliation, even when our disappointments are valid. Generosity means that we look for the best in every teen we work with and that we are patient with them throughout the entire struggle, helping their talents emerge. Generosity means we see the teen as central to every single interaction. Generosity means having a sense of humor about ourselves and our shortcoming and a willingness to allow for imperfections in ourselves and in others without defensiveness or shame.

IV

Forgiveness: means having the strength of character never to try to get even with a young person when things do not go very well or when the young person has somehow disappointed you. Forgiveness means having the personal capacity to explore unpleasant circumstances with the teens themselves, listening to what they have to say, saying what you have to say, and making the incident a thing of the past. Forgiveness means there is an acknowledgment that we are all imperfect, that having human flaws is not shameful or weak, and that people can turn a weakness into a strength. Forgiveness means that no matter what happens, the young person never doubts that he or she is very important to us. It means never turning our backs on them. No matter what occurs, forgiveness ensures that we are always there.

IV

Affectionate Action: is the combination of all of our gentleness, generosity and forgiveness in our work with young people. Being affectionately active means that the teens we encounter every day know that we care about them as individuals, despite imperfections. We teach ourselves not to be hot and cold with them, only giving warmth when they comply with our wishes. No, we must never withhold support or affection as a sign of disapproval or disappointment; this is an immature tactic, an attempt to control. Most young people are familiar with the withdrawal of affection; it is a common adult strategy, but if we employ it, they will stop trusting us and will resist all the more. What young people need from us is break-through behaviors and breakthrough modeling infused with our genuine caring for them.

IV

IV

HOLD WITH A RELEASING GRIP

In your work with teens, you must be their guide not their God. You probably do this all the time: anticipate their direction, offer tips to make their path a safer one, revise the map when necessary, encourage a steady route. For a time, you go along on the journey, illuminating pot-holes, warning about pitfalls, assessing short cuts; you offer an arm to steady them on the course.

But hold on to each young person with a releasing grip, because soon they will need to travel alone. You will have helped them learn how to negotiate the many detours and barriers they face. You will have been there striding along side, helping them develop confidence and hope. Soon enough, though, they will want to make their own way, perhaps even becoming a guide for someone else.

Help them walk this path, but stand back and

IV

watch when they take off. Some even learn to fly, surpassing what you have taught.

Be mindful of this: they may never have felt the path under their feet or the wind beneath them if you had not been their guide.

IV

IV

GO BACK ONCE MORE:
THAT'S WHEN THE MIRACLE OCCURS

Many young people in our work are accustomed to being rejected and abandoned both emotionally and physically. It may have first started in their homes, in their extended families, and then, for a variety of reasons, was repeated by teachers, counselors, and youth workers. Abandonment becomes such a regular feature of life, that for some, it seems to characterize all relationships with adults. Someone is always doing a disappearing act, turning a back, not showing up. Have you ever been faced with a teen whose behavior actually facilitated and accelerated rejection? It's almost as if the young person wanted to verify his or her expectation and get the whole thing over with.

Faced with such a teen, perhaps even a huge caseload of them, many adults in our field take the bait and respond in a rejecting way. How much easier it is to just move on to the next case, to act with repudiation, and to forget the pain of this particularly difficult teen. But, in doing so, we make ourselves part of the cycle, and who do you think suffers the consequences once again? And who do we blame for starting the whole thing? Who do we say precipitated this series of events, forcing us to turn away?

IV

I have done it myself.

But consider this as one of the most important lessons you will ever learn in this work: never turn your back on a young person. Never withdraw or withhold what you can still offer; when it all seems hopeless, go back one more time because that's when the miracle occurs. No doubt you will have to overcome your own hurt feelings or control issues, your own sense of righteousness; after all, you are only trying to help and this teen doesn't seem interested, or that one is insulting. But try to believe and continuously remind yourself that going back – just that one more time – is the time when the miracle might occur. That unbelievably magical, turn-around point may be reached with just one more approach, one more good deed, one more offer of help.

After you've done so much work, helped to make such important change, after you've been gentle and generous and forgiving, why would you give up now? Don't you want to be there when the miracle occurs? You are part of that miracle, so don't refuse to go back one more time; otherwise, you might miss it. What a shame that would be!

IV

IV

TEENS NEED TIME

Among the many complaints of people who work with teens is that there never seems to be enough time to get the job done. However, having "enough time" is key to succeeding in this precious work. Time is our currency with young people; if not us, who has time for them? In order for teens to get what they need, we must make the time to spend with them; we must give them time.

Often our face-to-face time with young people is constrained by external limits: a counseling session lasts only so long; a school period is 45 minutes or less; our case-management meetings or individual check-ins are often interrupted by other staff members, important phone calls, or paper work we need to get done. Because of these external pressures and scheduling limits, we never seem to reach the core interaction with the young person. It seems we rarely get to ask the important question, to find out what is really going on, or to inquire about how the teen is feeling. Then it does appear that we do not have enough time to get down to it.

Add these external time constraints to some of the common personal reactions youth workers sometimes have, and the problem clearly escalates. How many times do you think, "I don't have all day, here," when faced with a troubled adolescent who cannot quite articulate concisely the problem he or she is having or who appears to be wasting time with distracting behaviors? How many times have you thought, "I just don't have time for this," when perhaps all those deflecting behaviors are precisely how young people can communicate that they need you to pay attention, to take some time, to give them a minute, even if you think you couldn't find one in your day if you tried?

When we properly manage time, we prepare ahead by reading intake assessments and other background information in order to explore the core issues when the meeting begins. Ask yourself this question: did you spend as much time planning your class, meeting, counseling sessions with teens as you spent organizing your weekly or daily calendar? Did you spend a couple of minutes challenging yourself to come up with ideas for new interventions and strategies to help the young person? Did you attend to teens in the same painstaking fashion that you would when resolving your own issues or those of your child?

When you are together do teens get time with the full you – the creative, compassionate worker dedicated to improving the lives of young people?

Use your discretionary time to prepare for your meetings, so that even if you don't have all day, you can use each twenty-minute session, each half hour, efficiently. Twenty minutes of focused time is usually enough to get down to it with the young person sitting in front of you.

Take off your watch; now hold it in front of you.

Take a look at the time on your hands; it is what young people desperately need.

IV

IV

IV

LET THEM WIN

There's nothing better for a teen than leaving a session with you or your group feeling that something positive and affirming has just occurred. Such an ethos must characterize your work with young people, so that an uplifting, reassuring relationship can be formed. Their recognition of an adult's positive feelings and desire to help will bring teens back again and again.

Think of your new mantra as, "I will not let this teen go home if our business is unfinished, or if he or she is unhappy."

This is what a young person needs in order to build self-worth. It is important to understand that just because teens win (and should win) in interactions with us, we do not lose. In fact, we win too. This approach helps create a pleasant relationship, instead of those frequent acrimonious conversations and disapproving exchanges. It is not uncommon for young people to become "turned off" by an adult who cultivates an adversarial relationship, wrought with power struggles and disappointment.

Faced with tense and embattled relationships, some young people just stop showing up. Others will fight until the end, even if they are outnumbered, low on resources, and facing an unfair match. Adults almost always have all the fire-power, but some teenagers are so used to unfair fights, that they gear up, anyway, prepared for battle.

Nothing good comes of these wars. The next time you feel you are behind enemy lines, let the young person win.

You'll see the difference immediately.

IV

IV

SOMEONE MUST BE THE ADULT: THAT'S YOU

Working with teens in any setting frequently creates an environment of tension and stress. Inevitably there are pulls and tugs, stops and starts, tests and limits of power, heat and not much light. It is during these times that you will face your greatest challenge as a youth worker, a counselor, a teacher, a minister, and a parent. Sometimes a mistaken assumption or a misunderstanding kindles an unproductive, incendiary mood. Other times it is what we said, what they said, what we didn't say, or what they ought to have said. It is usually easy to predict when an exchange is taking a tense turn. But even when a young person clearly expresses antagonism, provokes hostility, or is utterly silent, we must always be the grown up.

Periodically, it is just such a hostile moment when the young person needs us the most. This may

IV

be difficult to understand since all overt evidence points toward the contrary. But I have learned in my almost forty years of working with teenagers, that this is exactly when they want to see calmness, evenhandedness, and fairness; they need it. This is exactly the moment when we must be the adult.

Most adolescents in our daily work feel that in life, they have lost, and adults have won. Adults, after all, have their own lives; they have so many resources to use against young people: sanctions, power, and other weapons. Using adult authority as our principal tool during difficult times does little to develop a context where aide and caring can flourish. It is important to remember that during such difficulties, young people need a lifeguard's hand, not an adversary's punch. Remaining stable, confident, and unprovoked is the only way to handle those times when tension runs hot and high.

I am reminded of numerous occasions in my early years as a school and community reproductive health worker when I learned that a young person, a thirteen or fourteen year old, had begun having sexual intercourse. In my mind's eye, I can still see myself, sitting there, saying, "Well, you have taken a big step by making this decision; I hope you know what you're doing. I sure hope you can handle this responsibility. What can I say? Let me know if I can help you in any way."

I know now that those words did some damage: that was the moment when I was needed most, and what did I offer but self-serving, distancing jargon. My attitude would never facilitate engagement or prove that I was someone who could help when and if help was needed. My response should have

IV

IV

been compassion and openness; I should have given that young person my schedule with time for our regular meetings. I should have been gentle and generous in my offer, no matter what.

In order to maintain engagement, to remain involved in the life decisions of teens with whom we work, we must not judge — neither overtly nor subtly. We must never judge. Surely, adult disappointment and disapproval abound in the lives of young people. Isn't it time to be the adult who understands? What a gift to teens to be the adult who understands when they behave in ways we hoped they wouldn't.

Remember this: safety, gentleness, and forgiveness.

Young people frequently forget what you say or do, but they rarely forget how you made them feel.

IV

IV

LOOKING AT TEENS: HOW TO READ THE SIGNS

Adolescents can be defined this way: a large hand (a very large hand) held with the palm facing out, in the STOP position, and next to it, a small hand (a very small hand), waving us on, beckoning us closer. The hands are contradicting each other in every way like opposite magnetic force fields. But have you ever noticed that most of us — teachers, youth workers, parents, counselors — pay more attention to the larger STOP sign?

"Stay away."

"Get off my back."

"You don't understand."

Such powerful messages stop us in our tracks, drain us of our vigor, and dampen our passion to help. They create barriers which seem almost insurmountable.

But if you look closely you will notice that

at the same time, there is a more obscured signal, often indirectly delivered. The teen is also quietly saying:

"I want to feel safe."

"I need you."

"I want to know the limits."

"I'm afraid."

"Don't go away."

These are powerful messages, too, but they are usually subtle because young people are in the midst of a difficult struggle to become independent and to be accepted by peers.

It is essential that we learn to read all the signs – there are usually many, and, at the very least, there are always two. Whenever you think you see just one big "No trespassing" signal, just one stern, "Leave me alone," look for the other message. It is there, but do not expect it to be expressed openly,

IV

since developmentally this type of admission makes teens feel too vulnerable. Nonetheless, just because they do not overtly say, "Don't worry, I'm listening," doesn't mean they aren't open to our lessons and caring.

Grown-ups do not always have realistic expectations of teens; we must take teens where they are, not where we want them to be. Think of the young person as shaking his or her head no, but at the same time as shouting in a quiet voice about his or her needs, hopes, dreams, and desires.

Listen for the quiet shouting, too.

Pay attention to all the signs.

IV

IV

BY ALL MEANS, RESUSCITATE

Many teachers, counselors and youth workers see the words "Do not resuscitate" written all over the young people with whom they work. The stunning reality of this unpardonable view is that young people – your students and clients – know when they are seen in such a way. The more rules, regulations, and requirements you create, the more expendable teens feel. They learn quickly that their needs are not your true concern, that they do not count for much in your equation.

IV

Young people have tremendously sensitive antenna that absorb our attitudes. They know how to interpret our looks, body posture, and language. They know when we are focused and when we are distracted; they know when we are just "doing our job," going through the motions, not offering eye contact, but instead eyeing our date books. They feel it personally when we take telephone calls and allow interruptions to shift our attention. The real-life drama in our lives communicate to young people that we do not care.

Paradoxically, these messages are the very ones most teens are looking out for. With indelible memories of lousy treatment by adults, young people are fluent in the language of rejection. Understanding that their needs are not anyone's emergency, many young people compete for adult attention. Others may respond with: "Well, they don't care about me," or "Why should I listen to what they say?" These reactions are often seen as needy, hostile, or ungrateful, rather than as natural reactions to the treatment they are receiving from us.

So much is at stake when we listen to young people and respond with generosity and genuine attention. There is meaning in each conversation. Therefore, make each one count for something.

Make each interaction a deposit, not a withdrawal. Let every conversation reverberate with your passion about their well-being, with your commitment to them. Provide the guidance and care they need. By doing this, you resuscitate, you breathe life.

IV

A GLOSSARY OF CONCEPTS

V

U

IMPORTANT CONCEPTS

Our best thinking and our best programs

got us here today. Look around. Is it acceptable?

———

Providing sexuality education is giving

information not making recommendations.

V

———

Talking about sexuality does not stimulate hormones,

create sexual interest, or provide permission.

Orthodox approaches have been enshrined,

but have they helped young people?

———

The problems we face in our work with young people

have taken the elevator;

our responses have taken the stairs.

———

After all is said and done,

much is said and little is done.

If you do what you've always done,

you'll get what you've always gotten –

is that good enough?

———

The world of young people is not

the world you remember.

———

Life's mountain top work is helping another person

have a better life.

V

V

Orthodoxy has failed.

It's time to be daring. Take risks.

Without changing no change will occur.

Effective programs for young people and families do not

happen by spontaneous combustion;

someone has got to light the fire.

Be incendiary in your efforts.

Our job is to help teens develop roots to grow

wings to fly.

———

Hold them with a releasing grip.

———

Self-esteem is caught not taught.

U

Remedial self-esteem enhancement takes years.

———

Desire, not improved cognition,

produces positive outcomes in teens.

———

When it comes to young people,

believe that all things are possible.

Desire produces delays in intercourse.

Desire produces conscientious contraceptive use.

Desire produces impulse control.

Desire reduces risk-taking.

V

Fundamental change in a young person's life

may be only one good deed away.

———

The more requirements that

have to be met before we help young people,

the more expendable they feel.

———

Expect the best from young people;

they're capable of it.

Young people frequently forget what you say and do,

but they rarely forget how you make them feel.

———

Our job is to find the gift in each young person;

keep looking.

———

Bathe the program and your work with teens in

the waters of "Yes you can."

It is difficult for young people who

have suffered greatly to be motivated.

———

In our work, imposing limits and standards without

compassion is not a virtue.

———

The key to talking with young people is

listening to them.

See every young person as pure potential.

———

Never give up on a young person;

always go back one more time because

that is when the miracle may occur.

———

Never taking a risk with a young person is

the biggest risk of all.

Many adults who work with young people see "do not resuscitate" written all over them.

———

Be patient, tenacious; outlast them; have patient endurance.

———

Let's dignify our work with young people by using trained staff.

U

Have realistic expectations.

There are no quick fixes in this work,

we are overdrawn at the quick-fix bank.

There are no microwave solutions when

working with teens.

V

With young people and families who suffer,

interventions must be like exercise:

if you don't keep it up, it falls down.

Repetitions, repetitions, repetitions.

———

It may indeed take a whole village to raise a child,

but it also takes a whole lifetime.

———

During the most difficult problems and traumas

is when young people need us most.

When we experience tense times with young people,

someone must be the grown up; that's us.

———

Develop a program culture that produces assets,

achievements, and accomplishments.

———

Do not underestimate the power of genuinely caring.

ABOUT THE AUTHOR

Michael A. Carrera has spent almost forty years in the community working as an educator with young people and families. As Director of The Children's Aid Society, National Adolescent Sexuality and Pregnancy Prevention Training Center, Dr. Carrera trains staff from agencies interested in implementing his holistic, long-term adolescent pregnancy prevention model. He has received awards from Advocates for Youth, SIECUS, Columbia University, Planned Parenthood Sexuality Educators of America, and the American Association of Sex Educators, Counselors, and Therapists (ASSECT). Dr. Carrera, Thomas Hunter Professor Emeritus at Hunter College, is also an adjunct professor at Mount Sinai Medical School in New York City. This is his fifth book.

To Order *Lessons for Lifeguards* write to:

Donkey Press
P.O. Box 20583
New York, N.Y. 10021-0071

Bulk order discounts available

NOTES

NOTES

NOTES

NOTES

NOTES